USA Patriot Act: Antiterror Legislation

345.73 SCH

Scheppler, Bill

THE USA PATRIOT ACT

Antiterror Legislation in Response to 9/11

Bill Scheppler

The Rosen Publishing Group, Inc., New York

"Those who would give up essential liberty to purchase a little temporary safety deserve neither liberty nor safety." –Benjamin Franklin

Published in 2006 by The Rosen Publishing Group, Inc.
29 East 21st Street, New York, NY 10010

Library of Congress Cataloging-in-Publication Data

Scheppler, Bill.
The USA Patriot Act: antiterror legislation in response to 9/11/Bill Scheppler.–1st ed.
     p. cm.–(The Library of American laws and legal principles)
Includes bibliographical references and index.
ISBN 1-4042-0457-1 (library binding)
1. United States. Uniting and Strengthening America by Providing Appropriate Tools Required to Intercept and Obstruct Terrorism (USA PATRIOT ACT) Act of 2001–Juvenile literature. 2. Terrorism–Prevention–United States–Juvenile literature. 3. War on Terrorism, 2001–Law and legislation–United States–Juvenile literature. I. Title. II. Series.

KF9430.Z9S34 2005
345.73'02–dc22
                                                                    2004030690

Manufactured in the United States of America

On the cover: The main entrance of the United States Supreme Court building faces the U.S. Capitol in Washington, D.C. The marble statue on the right side of the entrance represents Authority of Law and was carved by James Earle Fraser. The male figure holds a sword and a tablet, on which is written the Latin word *Lex,* meaning "law."

CONTENTS

INTRODUCTION

On September 11, 2001, the United States of America was attacked at home by foreign terrorists. The terrorists who executed the attack arrived in the country prior to 9/11. They lived in the United States for a significant amount of time (some for more than a year) as they completed their plot to hijack commercial airliners. Although the terrorists used their real names and operated in plain view, U.S. intelligence and law enforcement personnel never located nor questioned any of the nineteen men who participated in the attack.

Immediately following the 9/11 atrocity, U.S. citizens and lawmakers demanded to know why the government did not uncover the terror plot and how the country could prevent future strikes. The answer to the first question was not fully known until July 2004 when a special investigative team, known as the 9/11 Commission, delivered an in-depth report on the attack. The answer to the second question was a collection of antiterror laws contained in a comprehensive piece of legislation entitled the USA Patriot Act.

This book examines details of the 9/11 plot and identifies inadequacies in U.S. intelligence collection and analysis that may have caused missed opportunities to unveil the plan. It introduces examples of efforts to combat terrorism through legislation and points to key

Terrorists hijacked American Airlines Flight 77 on September 11, 2001, and slammed it into the Pentagon, the U.S. Department of Defense's headquarters, killing 125 people in the building and 64 passengers on the plane. The vast majority of members in the U.S. Congress believed that national security and law enforcement officials needed new and strong laws to help them fight terrorism. On October 26, 2001, President George W. Bush signed the USA Patriot Act into law as one effort to combat the war on terrorism.

provisions in the USA Patriot Act, which was drafted to remedy intelligence pitfalls. Finally, it considers the controversy surrounding the USA Patriot Act: some claim that the act erodes civil liberties, and federal lawsuits have ruled sections of the act unconstitutional.

Although the USA Patriot Act became law just six weeks after 9/11, with broad support from both Democratic and Republican lawmakers, its future is uncertain. The history of this piece of legislation will help you understand how it came into existence and follow its path from there.

CHAPTER ONE

America Awakens to the Terrorist Threat

Prior to September 11, 2001, most Americans living in the United States felt safe from the threat of violent attacks by foreign parties. Many Americans had dismissed the 1993 bombing in the parking garage beneath New York City's World Trade Center as an isolated incident. After all, Ramzi Yousef, the mastermind behind the attack, was in prison serving a life sentence. Similarly, the U.S. Embassy bombings in Kenya and Tanzania in 1998 occurred too far away to seem truly threatening. And although the deaths of seventeen sailors in the suicide attack on the USS *Cole* in the Yemeni port of Aden on October 12, 2000, were a terrible loss, the warship was a military target, so why should American civilians worry?

What Americans might have worried about was the increasing frequency of anti-American terrorist strikes occurring around the world. Intelligence agents uncovered a record number of leads during the summer of 2001, indicating a major attack against the United States was imminent. But much of this information was still under investigation prior to September 11, and the very real threat of an attack on U.S. soil was invisible to the general public—until it became shockingly clear.

A suicide attack on the USS *Cole* left this gaping hole in the port side of the U.S. ship, one of the world's most advanced guided missile destroyers. Two suicide bombers, who had connections to the terrorist group Al Qaeda, rammed their small boat, which was loaded with explosives, into the *Cole* as it was refueling in the port of Aden. Seventeen sailors were killed, and thirty-nine others were injured in the attack. The October 12, 2000, attack on the *Cole* was not considered an act of terrorism because the ship was a military target.

9/11: A DEVASTATING ATTACK ON U.S. SOIL

On the morning of September 11, 2001, terrorists seized four commercial airliners over the skies of the eastern United States in nearly simultaneous hijackings: American Airlines Flight 11 and United Airlines Flight 175, both traveling from Boston's Logan Airport to Los Angeles International; American Airlines Flight 77, bound for Los Angeles from Dulles Airport in Washington, D.C.; and United

The hijacked United Airlines Flight 175 struck the south tower *(left)* of the World Trade Center and burst into flames on September 11, seventeen minutes after American Airlines Flight 11 slammed into the north tower. Less than two hours later, both towers had collapsed, killing about 3,000 people. The United States had never suffered such a bloody terrorist attack on its own soil.

Airlines Flight 93, on a routine flight from Newark, New Jersey, to San Francisco. The terrorists selected cross-country flights because they knew the planes' tanks would be filled to capacity with highly flammable jet fuel. The fuel would serve as a powerful explosive agent when the hijackers used the aircraft as missiles, flying them into occupied buildings packed with people.

At 8:46 AM local time, Flight 11 crashed into the north tower of the World Trade Center in New York City. Seventeen minutes later, Flight 175 crashed into the south tower. After taking control of Flight 77 over West Virginia, the hijackers turned that airplane back toward Washington, D.C., and plowed into the western block of the Pentagon. Flight 93 was also redirected toward Washington before a passenger uprising forced the terrorists to abort their mission and dive into an open field in Shanksville, Pennsylvania. No one on board the planes survived. By 10:30 AM, both of the World Trade Center's 110-story towers had collapsed, and approximately 3,000 people were dead. This number of casualties was the largest ever sustained by the United States as the result of a foreign strike within its own borders.

The destruction left in the wake of the attack was incomprehensible to both American citizens and millions of sympathizers around the world. However, equally shocking was the callous planning and patience that must have gone into crafting the plot. The hijackings were well organized and methodically executed. In fact, information obtained from radio communications, flight recorders, and telephone conversations with passengers and crew members indicates the terrorists acted almost identically on each of the four flights.

Within hours of the strike, U.S. intelligence analysts assessed that the hijackings were the work of Al Qaeda, a bold anti-American terrorist network. U.S. agents immediately launched investigations into the attack and began piecing together the details of the plot.

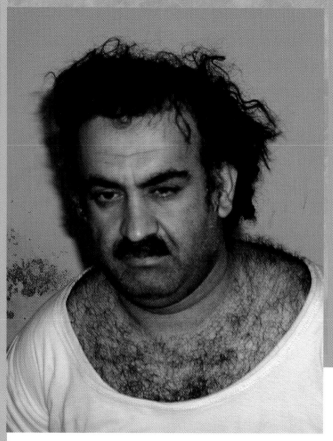

Khalid Sheikh Mohammed is considered to be the mastermind of 9/11. He is pictured here on March 1, 2003, after his capture in Rawalpindi, Pakistan. Mohammed was one of Osama bin Laden's top aides, and presented the plan for 9/11 to bin Laden in 1996.

FIVE YEARS OF PLANNING AND PREPARATION

Khalid Sheikh Mohammed, uncle of World Trade Center bomber Ramzi Yousef, had the original idea to hijack commercial airliners and use the planes as weapons in attacks on the United States. But his was a grand scheme, and to see it through, Mohammed needed financial support and personnel from an established organization. In 1996, he presented his plan to Al Qaeda leader Osama bin Laden and his chief of operations, Muhammad Atef. Bin Laden committed to backing the plot during a follow-up meeting in early 1999, six months after Al Qaeda conducted the Kenya and Tanzania bombings, which resulted in the deaths of 224 people.

Khalid Sheikh Mohammed took the lead in coordinating preparations for his plan. Bin Laden provided money to fund the plot, recruited and trained terrorist operatives to carry out the attack, and approved target selection to ensure that Al Qaeda objectives were addressed in the overall "statement" made by the strike. Mohammed and bin Laden agreed to target the World Trade Center, an icon of America's control over global finances; the

Pentagon, representing U.S. military strength and influence; and the U.S. Capitol, a symbol of U.S. domestic and foreign policy, which Al Qaeda viewed as pro-Israel and anti-Muslim. Mohammed and bin Laden made their strategic decisions from an Al Qaeda camp in Kandahar, Afghanistan. The terrorist operatives who executed the attack conducted the bulk of their logistical preparations in the United States.

FOREIGN TERRORISTS OPERATE IN PLAIN VIEW

All four terrorists who piloted the hijacked aircraft on 9/11 learned how to fly jets at flight schools inside the United States. Mohamed Atta, Marwan Al-Shehhi, and Ziad Jarrah were students and roommates in Hamburg, Germany, before they decided to travel to Chechnya and join the Islamic jihad against occupying Russian forces. During a stopover in Afghanistan, the three Muslim fundamentalists joined Al Qaeda and were recruited for the 9/11 plot by Atef, who valued their intelligence, fluency in English, and familiarity with Western culture. Atef sent the operatives back to Europe to enroll in flight school, but the men soon learned they could earn their pilots' licenses more cheaply and quickly at U.S. flight schools. In May and June 2000, the three terrorists arrived in Florida and began taking flying lessons.

Hani Hanjour was already a licensed pilot when he joined Al Qaeda in mid-2000. He received his initial flight training in Phoenix, Arizona, in the late 1990s after studying English at the University of Arizona. This experience qualified Hanjour as the ideal fourth and final pilot in the hijacking plot. By December 2000, Hanjour was back in the United States, brushing up on his piloting skills at a flight school in Mesa, Arizona.

In addition to the pilots, fifteen Al Qaeda-trained "muscle hijackers" participated in the September 11, 2001, attack. These men stormed the cockpits, killed the flight crews, and subdued the

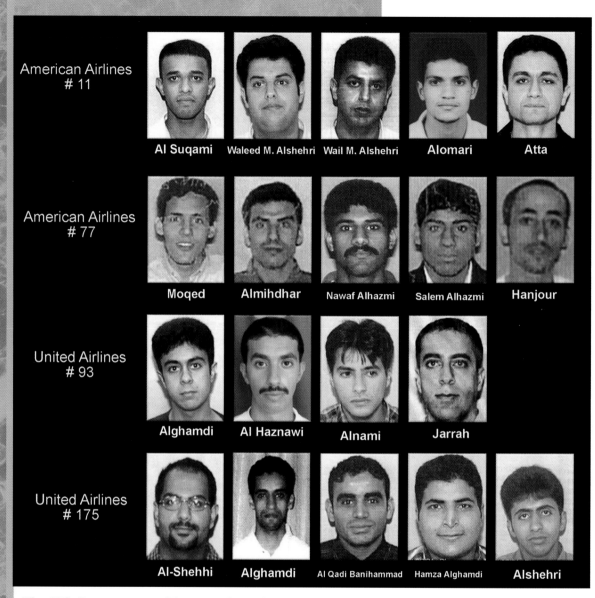

American Airlines # 11: Al Suqami, Waleed M. Alshehri, Wail M. Alshehri, Alomari, Atta

American Airlines # 77: Moqed, Almihdhar, Nawaf Alhazmi, Salem Alhazmi, Hanjour

United Airlines # 93: Alghamdi, Al Haznawi, Alnami, Jarrah

United Airlines # 175: Al-Shehhi, Alghamdi, Al Qadi Banihammad, Hamza Alghamdi, Alshehri

The U.S. Department of Justice released these pictures and names of the suspected hijackers on September 27, 2001. Mohamed Atta, Marwan Al-Shehhi, Ziad Jarrah, and Hani Hanjour, the terrorists who piloted the hijacked planes, all studied flying in the United States. The 9/11 plan required trained pilots who were willing to die in the attack, and synchronized techniques in hijacking the planes.

passengers while the pilots flew the planes. By April 2001, all nineteen terrorists who would take part in the strike were living in the United States and making tactical preparations. For the pilots, this meant taking cross-country flights on the exact type of aircraft they would hijack, sitting in the same sections they would sit in on September 11. During these flights, they identified the ideal time to begin the attacks and the types of weapons they could successfully bring on board. The muscle hijackers prepared by working out in local gyms.

The final phase of preparation was spent studying airline schedules to synchronize flight times and to select a date. This step was left to Mohamed Atta. Atta chose four flights with similar departure times to ensure the hijackings would occur as simultaneously as possible. He picked a date after the first week in September–when the U.S. Congress returned from its summer break–guaranteeing that the Capitol would be occupied. Upon final approval from Khalid Sheikh Mohammed and bin Laden, Atta coordinated the reservation of nineteen airline tickets, which were purchased between August 25 and September 5.

CHAPTER TWO
Counterterrorism Intelligence Failures

Four years after 9/11, following hundreds of interviews and countless hours of investigation, U.S. government officials know quite a bit about the operation. They know the identities and backgrounds of all nineteen participants. They know when most of these individuals arrived in the United States, where they stayed, and a great deal about their activities while they were in the country. These officials also know about the terrorist network behind the attack, the men who masterminded the plot, and how it was funded. But how much of this information did the U.S. government know prior to the attack?

In retrospect, the United States may have had enough intelligence prior to 9/11 to prevent the strike—either directly, by exposing the plot and detaining its participants, or indirectly, by getting close enough to persuade its planners to call it off. However, the information was fragmented across multiple intelligence agencies. These agencies in turn employed their own counterterrorism divisions and rarely collaborated in their investigation efforts. As a result, no single agency had enough information to launch an effective probe into the threat—until it was too late.

On August 7, 1998, the U.S. embassies in Nairobi, Kenya, and Dar es Salaam, Tanzania, were bombed within five minutes of each other by followers of Osama bin Laden. In response, on August 20, 1998, President Bill Clinton ordered a cruise missile attack on a terrorist training center in Afghanistan that was linked to Al Qaeda. The CIA and FBI each had intelligence about the Al Qaeda bombing operatives. If shared, that intelligence might have led the agencies to scrutinize the men when they entered the United States with visas.

ALHAZMI AND AL-MIDHAR SLIP INTO THE UNITED STATES

In December 1999, the Central Intelligence Agency (CIA) and its Counterterrorist Center (CTC) received information that men connected with Al Qaeda and the U.S. Embassy bombings in Kenya and Tanzania were planning to meet in Kuala Lumpur, Malaysia. By the time the meeting took place in January 2000, one of the men had been identified as Khalid Al-Midhar. The CIA reported this information to the Federal Bureau of Investigation (FBI) but continued to keep the investigative lead on the meeting, agreeing to alert the FBI again if a domestic concern developed. Later that month, the CIA learned that Al-Midhar possessed a U.S. visa, which is a travel document that grants entry into the United States. This information qualified as a domestic concern, but the FBI was not informed.

In March 2000, a second participant in the Kuala Lumpur meeting was identified. The CIA received intelligence that Nawaf Alhazmi attended the meeting and then traveled to Bangkok, Thailand, before boarding a United Airlines flight to Los Angeles on January 15, 2000. Alhazmi also held a U.S. visa. Again, the FBI was not alerted.

As it turned out, Alhazmi and Al-Midhar were the first two 9/11 hijackers to enter the United States, traveling together on the January 15 flight. (Bin Laden originally assigned Alhazmi and Al-Midhar as pilots in the plot, but because the men never completed flight training, they participated as muscle hijackers.) The CIA was on the right track in investigating the Kuala Lumpur meeting and identifying these men as potential Al Qaeda operatives. Unfortunately, they lost their trail in Malaysia and did not share intelligence updates with the FBI. Had the FBI been aware that these men had visas granting entry into the United States, it may have been prepared to continue the investigation upon their arrival.

THE CIA MISSES A GOLDEN OPPORTUNITY

One year after the Kuala Lumpur meeting, a third participant was positively identified. The FBI and CIA were each conducting investigations of the October 2000 bombing of the USS *Cole*. In December 2000, an FBI informant identified Tawfiq bin Attash (aka Khallad) as the mastermind behind the strike. In January 2001, the same informant provided the CIA with intelligence placing Khallad at the Kuala Lumpur meeting with Al-Midhar and Alhazmi. This intelligence connected two potential terrorists who had access to

Nawaf Alhazmi's name is listed in this San Diego, California, telephone book. The CIA had information about Alhazmi's attendance at the Kuala Lumpur meeting, but did not alert the FBI about his holding a U.S. visa. Alhazmi flew to Los Angeles, and moved to an apartment in San Diego. Alhazmi was one of the hijackers of American Airlines Flight 77 that attacked the Pentagon on 9/11.

the United States, with a senior Al Qaeda official who had already executed a deadly attack against a U.S. target. Because the CIA was concentrating on the *Cole* bombing, not a possible strike in the United States, it did not follow up on this connection. And it did not share the new lead with the FBI.

Al-Midhar was not in the United States when this new intelligence became available. He had left in June 2000 and traveled to Yemen (where he may have played a role in the *Cole* bombing). The U.S. State Department maintains a TIPOFF watch list of known and suspected terrorists. The list is used by U.S. immigration and border patrols to deny entry of terrorists into the United States. The CIA

Kuala Lumpur's Petronas Towers and Asy-Syakirin Mosque are pictured here around 2000. U.S. intelligence officials did not realize until the summer of 2002 that the terrorists' meeting in January 2000 in Kuala Lumpur was to plan the Al Qaeda attack on the USS *Cole* and 9/11.

could have registered Al-Midhar's name on the TIPOFF list in January 2000, based on his Al Qaeda ties and U.S. visa, or in January 2001, when U.S. officials discovered his connection with Khallad. Had Al-Midhar's name been on the list, he likely would have been identified and detained for questioning when applying for a new U.S. visa in June 2001 or upon arrival in New York on the Fourth of July.

BARRIERS TO INTELLIGENCE COMMUNICATION

In May 2001, it appeared as though the CIA and the FBI might finally work together to recognize the threat Al-Midhar posed to national security. An FBI analyst working on the *Cole* investigation had information that Al Qaeda operative Fahd Al-Quso transferred money to Khallad in Bangkok in January 2000 and may have attended the Kuala Lumpur meeting. She received surveillance photos of the meeting from a CIA analyst and presented them to a team of FBI agents (who were also working on the *Cole* case and had previously interviewed Al-Quso) in hopes of obtaining a positive identification.

All the intelligence required to mount an investigation into Al-Midhar was in the room during this presentation. The CIA agent

Former White House counterterrorism adviser Richard A. Clarke testified before the 9/11 Commission on March 24, 2004. Clarke said that, in his opinion, President George W. Bush's administration made the war against terrorism an important issue but not an urgent one, and that it could have worked harder to prevent the 9/11 attacks. The Bush administration responded that Clarke's testimony was contradictory, because in the fall of 2002, Clarke had praised the president's antiterrorism efforts in internal memos.

On March 24, 2004, George Tenet, then director of the Central Intelligence Agency, testified before the 9/11 Commission that the CIA told President Bush and his senior officials before they took office in January 2001 that Osama bin Laden was a threat to the United States.

could have identified Khallad, Al-Midhar, and Alhazmi in the photographs to establish a clear Al Qaeda connection. Further, he could have disclosed the likelihood that Al-Midhar and Alhazmi were either traveling to or already in the United States based on their visas and Alhazmi's flight to Los Angeles. The FBI analyst had information from a National Security Agency (NSA) report that tied Al-Midhar to a suspected terrorist facility in the Middle East. The team of FBI agents had intelligence linking that same facility to the U.S. Embassy bombings.

Unfortunately, the analysts' interpretation of the Foreign Intelligence Surveillance Act (FISA) prohibited them from communicating this information to one another. FISA established standards for collecting foreign intelligence that differ from the standards applied to criminal investigations. Because the *Cole* case was a criminal investigation and the photographs were taken as part of a foreign intelligence mission, the analysts believed that information on the Kuala Lumpur meeting could not be shared with the FBI agents, no matter how many questions they asked. Two days after the presentation, Al-Midhar picked up his new visa.

CHAPTER THREE

Fighting Terror Through Legislation

Prior to September 11, 2001, most Americans viewed the bombings of the World Trade Center, the U.S. embassies in Kenya and Tanzania, and the USS *Cole* as individual acts of terror against U.S. targets. But intelligence reports proved that these incidents were directly related, and the terrorists responsible for them were evolving in both confidence and sophistication. In the days and weeks following 9/11, this intelligence prompted burning questions directed at U.S. lawmakers: "What could we have done to prevent 9/11? How do we protect ourselves from future attack?"

Questions such as these arise any time a tragic event draws the national spotlight, and often the answers come in the form of new laws. U.S. antiterror legislation has been evolving for decades. The laws passed in the wake of 9/11 were inspired in part by the Al Qaeda hijackings, but they were also extensions of existing antiterror legislation. The common thread among these laws is an attempt by Congress to empower intelligence agents and law enforcement personnel to effectively protect the American public and U.S. interests at home and abroad.

This chapter describes the evolution of U.S. antiterror legislation beginning with the Foreign Intelligence Surveillance Act of 1978.

Senator Patrick Leahy of Vermont, the ranking Democrat on the Senate Judiciary Committee, speaks at a press conference in February 2003. The committee charged the FBI and the Justice Department with employing too much secrecy, having insufficient training, having weak information analysis, and suppressing internal dissent in the use of the Foreign Intelligence Surveillance Act.

THE FOREIGN INTELLIGENCE SURVEILLANCE ACT

The Foreign Intelligence Surveillance Act (FISA) was passed in 1978 to provide additional freedom to U.S. intelligence agencies that collect information on foreign powers and agents of foreign powers. Prior to FISA, no distinction existed between the rules regulating information collection in a criminal case against an American citizen and surveillance of a foreign terrorist scheming to strike a U.S. target. The Fourth Amendment to the U.S. Constitution guarantees American citizens protection against unlawful search and seizure by government agents. This includes reading mail, wiretapping telephones, and entering homes without a warrant. Foreign powers under surveillance benefited from these same constitutional protections. But in the Cold

Does the Government Know You're Reading This Book?

If an FBI agent *suspects* that a person poses a national security threat, Section 215 of the Patriot Act allows that agent to solicit "tangible things" about that suspect from any third party. One item covered in Section 215 is personal information that libraries have on record about you. Maybe you want to learn more about 9/11. Suppose you check out a copy of the Koran (the holy book of Islam); a tourist guide on Malaysia, so you can identify Kuala Lumpur; and a flight-training manual, to show how challenging it was to learn to fly a commercial jet so quickly. What would your library record tell the FBI about you? Would you be suspected of planning a similar plot?

War era, when there was a demand for more leeway to investigate members of the Communist Party, protection for foreign powers was challenged by FISA.

FISA broadly defined a foreign power as anything from a foreign nation to a corporation controlled by a foreign nation to a political organization not substantially composed of American citizens. An international terrorist organization such as Al Qaeda would certainly fall into this category. Under FISA, U.S. intelligence agencies could place a foreign power under surveillance without evidence of criminal activity or intent as long as "the primary purpose" of surveillance was to collect federal intelligence. FISA permitted electronic eavesdropping, wiretapping, public tracking, and photography as acceptable surveillance methods. In 1994, lawmakers extended FISA to allow secret entry into buildings as part of security investigations.

Rescue workers pick through the debris at the Alfred P. Murrah Federal Building in Oklahoma City, Oklahoma, in April 1995. Timothy McVeigh rented a truck, packed it with explosives, and detonated it in front of the government office building, killing 168 people. After the bombing, Congress passed the Antiterrorism and Effective Death Penalty Act in 1996 to enable law enforcement officials to investigate and prosecute terrorist attacks on U.S. citizens.

ANTITERRORISM AND EFFECTIVE DEATH PENALTY ACT OF 1996

Many of the laws making up the Antiterrorism and Effective Death Penalty Act (ATA) were drafted following the 1993 World Trade Center bombing but had not passed through Congress because antiterror legislation was a relatively low priority at the time. That changed with the 1995 bombing of the Alfred P. Murrah Federal Building in Oklahoma City, Oklahoma. Americans found the Murrah attack particularly distressing because it took place in an unassuming midwestern city and 19 of the 168 people who died were children attending the building's Child Development Center. Riding the wave of public outrage, the ATA passed Congress with bipartisan support and became law on April 24, 1996.

Key ATA legislation addressing financial restrictions on terrorist funding, stronger immigration laws, extended international jurisdiction, and increased resources and tools to fight terrorism were available to intelligence analysts prior to 9/11. These antiterrorism measures remain relevant after 9/11.

Title III of the ATA uses U.S. global financial strength as leverage to control the funding of organizations that support terrorists and to sever aid to any country associated with terrorist activities. Title IV authorizes the rejection of U.S. visas to foreign citizens on the basis of membership in a recognized terrorist organization. Further, it eases barriers to deporting suspected terrorists, while protecting the classified information used to determine the foreigner's terrorist status. Extending U.S. law enforcement jurisdiction, Title VII enables agents to investigate and prosecute terrorists involved in international attacks against U.S. citizens and targets without relying on local governments. And Title VIII prescribes increased funding of antiterrorism efforts for everything from personnel to technology.

A CALL FOR NEW LEGISLATION FOLLOWING 9/11

On September 12, 2001, U.S. Justice Department officials met to define the problems that may have contributed to the inability of intelligence and law enforcement personnel to detect and prevent the 9/11 hijackings. The goal of the meeting was to draft guidelines for new legislation that would address these problems and hopefully protect the United States from future attack. The group received staunch direction from U.S. attorney general John Ashcroft: draft a proposal that provides "all that is necessary for law enforcement, within the bounds of the Constitution."

On September 12, 2001, President George W. Bush, his cabinet, the Joint Chiefs of Staff, and his National Security Team met to discuss U.S. antiterrorism strategies after the September 11, 2001, attacks. Justice Department officials also met on that day to set into motion proposals for new legislation to address intelligence and law enforcement efforts in the war against terrorism.

Attorney General Ashcroft was equally demanding of the U.S. Congress, insisting both the House of Representatives and the Senate approve the Justice Department's plan within a week. It was clear that U.S. president George W. Bush and his administration believed law enforcement should be granted as much authority as possible as quickly as possible to locate and apprehend the terrorists responsible for the 9/11 attack. Members of the House and the Senate shared the Bush administration's desire and had already begun drafting their own antiterror legislation.

CHAPTER FOUR

The USA Patriot Act Becomes Law

The USA Patriot Act is a combination of several pieces of legislation, most notably the State Department proposal, Senate bill S. 1510, and House of Representatives bill H.R. 2975. Its name, too, is a hybrid, bringing together the titles of the competing legislation. "USA Patriot" is an acronym that stands for Uniting and Strengthening America by Providing Appropriate Tools Required to Intercept and Obstruct Terrorism, but this law is most commonly referred to as the Patriot Act.

President Bush's requirements for post-9/11 antiterror legislation were addressed by the State Department proposal and included three main areas of focus: information gathering and sharing, criminal law and procedure, and border protection and immigration procedure. Although the president's influence is evident in both congressional bills, members of the House and the Senate fought hard to strike a balance between increasing the power of intelligence and law enforcement personnel and eroding civil liberties including the right to privacy granted to all American citizens. In the end, after a joint congressional committee achieved a compromise, both houses passed the bill. President Bush signed it into law just six weeks after the 9/11 atrocity.

President George W. Bush signed the USA Patriot Act into law during a ceremony at the White House a little more than six weeks after the 9/11 attack. The act gives police authority to secretly search homes and business records and to eavesdrop on telephone and computer conversations.

CONGRESS COLLABORATES ON A BIPARTISAN BILL

On October 2, 2001, U.S. representative James Sensenbrenner, a Republican from Wisconsin, introduced H.R. 2975 to the House of Representatives for review. Three days later, Judiciary Committee leader Senator Patrick Leahy, a Democrat representing the state of Vermont, submitted S. 1510 to the U.S. Senate. Representative Sensenbrenner worked primarily with his fellow representatives, including John Conyers, a Michigan Democrat, and twenty-five other cosponsors to draft H.R. 2975. In the interest of time, Senator Leahy worked on S. 1510 directly with White House officials and members of the State Department to ensure the legislation addressed the needs of the Bush administration, thereby speeding the approval process. In the end, H.R. 2975 and S. 1510 were very similar in that they both substantially extended FISA authorities and other existing antiterror laws. The House bill, however, included two safeguards that the State Department would not support in Leahy's bill: a sunset clause, which would make the FISA extensions temporary; and a judicial review process, requiring intelligence agents to gain FISA court approval before executing surveillance campaigns.

The members of the House of Representatives put H.R. 2975 up for vote on October 12, and it passed handily with 337 votes for and 79 against. Meanwhile, S. 1510 had passed the Senate by a landslide margin of 96-1. With two strong bills in hand, Congress decided to consolidate both into a single new bill. The resulting bill was H.R. 3162, the USA Patriot bill. To the disappointment of White House officials, H.R. 3162 retained the sunset clause and judicial review safeguards. But another terrorist attack on October 17, in the form of an anthrax-contaminated letter sent to Senate Majority Leader Tom Daschle, forced the Bush administration to accept the bill as it was in order to pass the legislation immediately. H.R. 3162 was introduced to the House on October 23 and passed the next day by a vote of 357–66. It was presented to the Senate on October 24 and once again passed the next day, this time by a margin of 98–1. The approved bill was submitted to the White House that same day. President Bush signed the Patriot Act into law on October 26, 2001.

HOW THE PATRIOT ACT HELPS COMBAT TERRORISM

The Patriot Act is a lengthy collection of legislation that covers a broad range of antiterror laws across more than 300 pages. (See the For More Information section at the end of this book to find out where you can read the entire document online.) The following are some key provisions of the Patriot Act that are intended to directly assist intelligence and law enforcement personnel in their efforts to identify and prevent another terrorist plot like the September 11, 2001, attack.

Letter to Tom Brokaw

Letter to Senator Daschle

The Justice Department released these photographs of the envelopes that had been sent to NBC-TV anchor Tom Brokaw and Senate Majority Leader Tom Daschle in October 2001. The letters inside the envelopes contained spores of anthrax, the source of an infectious disease that can be fatal to humans. The letters were sent at the same time that Congress was debating and revising its USA Patriot bill.

THE SIGNIFICANCE OF "A SIGNIFICANT PURPOSE"

As explained earlier in this book, in chapter 3, FISA applied to surveillance of a foreign power or an agent of a foreign power as long as "the primary purpose" of surveillance is the gathering of foreign intelligence. This was the fundamental barrier to sharing information between intelligence collecting operations and criminal investigations. Section 218 of the Patriot Act amends FISA to allow its use in cases where foreign intelligence is "a significant purpose." This seemingly minor edit has a huge impact on the law. Had "a significant purpose" of monitoring the Kuala Lumpur meeting been foreign intelligence, then the CIA could have shared that information with the FBI agents investigating the USS *Cole* bombing as an additional, less significant purpose.

(Left) Zacarias Moussaoui, a French citizen of Moroccan descent, was a key figure in the September 11, 2001, attacks. He was indicted on December 11, 2001, by the U.S. Justice Department on six charges of conspiracy and faced the death penalty on four of the charges. Osama bin Laden allegedly had considered calling off the 9/11 attacks after Moussaoui's arrest in August. *(Right)* FBI director Robert Mueller, center, with Senator Pat Leahy, left, and Senator Chuck Grassley, entered a Senate Judiciary hearing in June 2002. Mueller stated that on May 30 he asked the inspector general of the Justice Department to investigate complaints by an FBI agent in Minneapolis, Minnesota, that the FBI had mishandled Moussaoui's case before the 9/11 attacks.

DETENTION PERIOD FOR SUSPECTED TERRORISTS

Section 412 permits mandatory detention up to seven days for any alien in the United States who poses a threat to national security. At the end of the detention period, a Justice Department official determines if criminal charges should be brought against the alien or if he or she will be deported to his or her country of origin. If in early 2000, the CIA had informed the FBI of Alhazmi's connection to Al Qaeda and flight to Los Angeles, this provision would have allowed the FBI to apprehend Alhazmi immediately upon detection.

Sunsetting the Patriot Act

Sixteen of the Patriot Act's provisions are scheduled to expire on December 31, 2005. Congress included this "sunset clause" in the bill because the original purpose of these provisions was to provide the tools necessary to capture the terrorists responsible for 9/11, not to permanently alter intelligence-collecting practices. Supporters of the Patriot Act argue that all 150 provisions are necessary to combat terrorism, and because the "war on terror" will likely continue beyond 2005, Congress should not allow any provisions to expire at that time. As a compromise, each provision will be reviewed by the Senate Judiciary Committee prior to December 31, and those found to be necessary beyond 2005 will be altered to avoid expiration.

According to Khalid Sheikh Mohammed, Osama bin Laden considered calling off the 9/11 plot when the FBI arrested a loosely connected associate, Zacarias Moussaoui, for an immigration violation in August 2001. Had the FBI captured Alhazmi (a key player at the time), it's possible the attack might have been avoided.

PEN REGISTERS AND TRAP AND TRACE DEVICES

Pen registers and trap and trace devices are telephone wiretapping tools that law enforcement personnel have employed in criminal investigations for many years. Pen registers track the telephone numbers dialed on outgoing calls, and trap and trace devices track the numbers of telephones initiating incoming calls. Section 216 of the Patriot Act amended the existing pen register and trap and trace law to include e-mail messages. The Patriot Act allows intelligence agents to capture outgoing and incoming e-mail addresses, without intercepting e-mail content or subject line text. This provision updates the original law, which was enacted in 1986 when computers were not seen as mass communication devices, but it would have played an insignificant role in uncovering the 9/11 plot. As FBI director Robert Mueller noted during a speech he gave in San

Francisco, California, on April 19, 2002, "The hijackers had no computers, no laptops, no storage media of any kind."

DELAYED WARRANT NOTIFICATION

With increased freedom and more tools to investigate foreign terrorist suspects, the chances that a suspect discovers that he or she is under surveillance also increase. This could result in his or her destroying evidence or fleeing the country. Delayed warrant notification masks the investigation in secrecy. In most criminal cases, when government agents execute a search warrant, they must provide a copy of the warrant at the time it is used. In Section 213, the Patriot Act specifies that a delay is permissible when immediate notice would have an adverse effect on the investigation. A judge determines the duration of the delay, after which time notice must be given to the suspect. Intelligence agents never got close enough to the 9/11 terrorists to need a search warrant, but the benefits of searching premises in secret are obvious.

CHAPTER FIVE

Balancing Safety with Civil Liberties

The general purpose of the Patriot Act is to make collecting information on suspected and potential terrorists easier for U.S. intelligence agents and law enforcement officials. The hope is that the more information the authorities possess on these people, the better the chance that the agents will identify terrorist attacks before they occur. Taken at face value, it is difficult to argue against this strategy. But many law experts and civil libertarians see potential for abuse in the additional surveillance freedoms granted by the Patriot Act.

In criminal investigations, a government official must show probable cause that a person has committed a crime or intends to do so to obtain warrants for searches and surveillance. In foreign intelligence cases, a government official must only convince the FISA court that a person is an agent of a foreign power—traditionally, FISA court approval has been significantly easier to obtain. In the year after President Bush signed the Patriot Act into law, FISA warrants increased from 934 to 1,228, while criminal warrants for similar access were down 9 percent. According to Beryl A. Howell, former general counsel for the Senate Judiciary Committee, these figures are directly related.

The concern is that if a government official is unable to obtain a warrant in a criminal case, he or she may attempt to make a loose connection between the suspect and a foreign power. The government official may argue that "a significant purpose" of the investigation is foreign intelligence collection to gain access to the surveillance tools specified in the Patriot Act. As Mary Broderick, executive director of California Attorneys for Criminal Justice, stated in a November 2001 interview with the *San Francisco Chronicle*, "I think the public is fooling itself if they think the government is going to limit its intrusion on civil liberties to those people who are legitimate suspects."

U.S. attorney general John Ashcroft holds a copy of a study entitled "Report from the Field: The USA Patriot Act at Work" in July 2004. The attorney general said that the act had enabled the intelligence community to share information in ways that were not possible before.

ORGANIZED OPPOSITION TO THE PATRIOT ACT

Across the United States, citizens opposed to some or all of the Patriot Act's provisions have gathered to challenge the law's constitutionality, most often citing violations of the First and Fourth Amendments to the U.S. Constitution. Among other guarantees, the First Amendment promises freedom to practice religion, but in the months following 9/11, this liberty became strained for Americans who practice Islam. U.S. intelligence agencies put hundreds of mosques under surveillance because all the terrorists involved in the plot were Muslim. By

Samina Faheem, executive director of American Muslim Voice, spoke during a protest against the USA Patriot Act in San Francisco, California, in July 2003. Some civil rights and community groups have joined to declare their opposition to the Domestic Security Enhancement Act, or Patriot Act II, which continued to work its way through congressional committees. The proposed act would grant the U.S. government broad powers to investigate, detain, and interrogate terrorist suspects.

tracking attendance and interaction at the mosques and cataloging this information, the government also infringed upon Fourth Amendment rights to privacy.

Mikal Condon, spokesperson for the Electronic Privacy Information Center, said in a November 2001 interview, "It's going to be a wait-and-see to see if the new powers are just used or abused. I'd cross your fingers and hope for the best." As of April 2005, more than 375 U.S. cities and five states had seen enough.

A Patriot Act Nightmare

On March 11, 2004, in an attack that became known as 3/11, terrorists bombed several commuter trains in Madrid, Spain. In the ensuing investigation, FBI agents determined that a fingerprint found on a bag containing explosives might have belonged to Brandon Mayfield of Oregon. Mayfield was a Muslim and an attorney who had indirect links to terrorists, which allowed the FBI to label him a foreign agent and unleash an investigation using all the tools of the Patriot Act. Agents searched Mayfield's home in his absence, tapped his phone, and held him in custody without pressing charges—even after Spanish authorities proved the fingerprint was not his. Mayfield was found not guilty and released, but his is an example of freedom's vulnerability under the Patriot Act.

Each of these communities passed resolutions declaring they would hold their citizens' constitutional rights above federal law in cases where government agents attempt to place their residents under surveillance in the name of the Patriot Act.

LAWSUITS CHALLENGING THE PATRIOT ACT

In July 2003, the American Civil Liberties Union (ACLU) filed the first lawsuit in federal court against the Patriot Act. In the lawsuit, the ACLU claimed Section 215 of the Patriot Act violates constitutional protections against unreasonable search and seizure as well as freedoms of speech and association. As of April 2005, this case was still pending, but two other federal court cases have resulted in rulings that found portions of the Patriot Act to be unconstitutional.

In January 2004, the Humanitarian Law Project (HLP) challenged Section 805 of the Patriot Act on behalf of several humanitarian groups and two U.S. citizens facing fifteen years in prison for assisting Kurds in Turkey. They had been accused of "giving advice or assistance to a group identified as a foreign terrorist organization" because the Kurds belonged to the Kurdistan Workers Party, which then secretary of state Madeleine Albright had identified

On the steps of Federal Hall in New York City, protesters demonstrated against the USA Patriot Act while Attorney General John Ashcroft visited the area in September 2003. Earlier in the day, Ashcroft had delivered a speech in which he defended the USA Patriot Act as a protector of American lives. Parts of the act are set to expire on December 31, 2005, unless Congress renews the legislation.

as a terrorist organization in 1997. U.S. District Court judge Audrey Collins ruled that section 805 of the Patriot Act was unconstitutional on the grounds that it violated the First and Fifth Amendments. The text, she found, did not distinguish between violent and nonviolent activities. The plaintiffs had been assisting Kurdish refugees through lawful support.

The second case, argued in front of U.S. District Court judge Victor Marrero in September 2004, challenged the constitutionality of Section 505. In this case, the plaintiff was an Internet service provider (ISP). The FBI contacted the ISP via a National Security

Letter (NSL) seeking customer e-mail and Internet activity records. The NSL indicated a secret search and even went as far as prohibiting the ISP from mentioning the letter. Judge Marrero found Section 505 to be in violation of the First and Fourth amendments. He ruled that the search was unreasonable because the ISP could take no action to challenge it and forbidding the ISP from mentioning the NSL defied freedom of speech.

LEGISLATIVE RESPONSES TO THE PATRIOT ACT

The future of the Patriot Act is in jeopardy. As federal courts hear more lawsuits, more components may be found unconstitutional. Portions of the Patriot Act are set to expire on December 31, 2005, as declared in the sunset clause, but Congress has the opportunity to vote to renew the act before the deadline. Moreover, the 9/11 Commission was assembled in November 2002 to conduct a comprehensive investigation into the terrorist attack and report back to Congress its recommendations for resolving breakdowns in intelligence gathering and sharing, which it did in July 2004. The passage of the Patriot Act is considered by many to have been a knee-jerk reaction to the 9/11 tragedy because something had to be done to make Americans feel safer. But the law was written in haste and hustled through Congress with limited understanding and even less debate. The Patriot Act is set to evolve into the next phase of U.S. antiterror legislation, and it will only benefit from the extensive recommendations of the 9/11 Commission report and a fully engaged legislative process.

GLOSSARY

Al Qaeda Arabic, meaning "the foundation." Al Qaeda is an independent military organization that is heavily influenced by its fundamental interpretation of the Islamic religion. Established by Osama bin Laden in 1988, it is a network of groups and is widely regarded as a terrorist organization.

Central Intelligence Agency (CIA) The United States' foreign intelligence agency. The CIA is responsible for obtaining and analyzing information about foreign powers and individuals, and reporting such information to the various branches of the U.S. government.

civil liberties Accepted rights that protect citizens from the power of a government. Examples in the United States include freedom of speech, freedom of assembly, and trial by jury, which are all documented in the U.S. Constitution.

Cold War The ideological and political "war" (1945–1990) between the United States and its allies and the Soviet Union. The Cold War was waged primarily by intelligence agencies and did not lead to direct combat. The two sides also supported opposing sides in conflicts in regions such as the Middle East, Southeast Asia, and Latin America.

embassy Permanent representation of one nation state in another nation state typically headed by an ambassador. In this book, embassy also refers to the building that houses the representatives, which is also known as a "chancery."

Federal Bureau of Investigation (FBI) The principal investigative arm of the Department of Justice. Among other missions, the FBI investigates violations of federal criminal law and protects the country from foreign intelligence and terrorist activities.

hijacking The forcible seizure or robbery of any vehicle in transit usually by an armed person or group. The takeover of an airplane is sometimes referred to as "skyjacking."

intelligence In this book, "intelligence" refers to the process and the result of gathering and analyzing information that is secret or difficult to obtain.

Islam Arabic word meaning "submission (to God)," Islam is described as a way of life and/or religion. Followers of Islam are known as Muslims, who practice the religious teachings of the prophet Muhammad that are contained in the Qur'an (Koran).

jihad Arabic word from the root *jahada*, which means "exerting utmost effort." Originally referring to domestic struggle for purity, it is commonly used by Muslims to describe an armed struggle against foreign occupation or oppression.

legislation The written laws of a government. In the United States, federal legislation is typically drafted and passed by Congress and then confirmed or signed into law by the president.

terrorism The calculated use of violence or the threat of violence against a civilian population for the purpose of producing fear, usually for some political end. An active participant in an act of terrorism is a terrorist.

World Trade Center (WTC) The WTC was a business complex in New York City dedicated to companies and organizations directly involved in "world trade." At the time the twin towers were completed (the north tower in 1972, and the south tower in 1973), they were the tallest buildings in the world.

FOR MORE INFORMATION

Central Intelligence Agency
Office of Public Affairs
Washington, DC 20505
Web site: http://www.cia.gov

Federal Bureau of Investigation
J. Edgar Hoover Building
935 Pennsylvania Avenue NW
Washington, DC 20535-0001
Web site: http://www.fbi.gov

United States Department of Justice
950 Pennsylvania Avenue NW
Washington, DC 20530-0001
Web site: http://www.usdoj.gov (for USA Patriot Act, see
http://www.lifeandliberty.gov)

Web Sites

Due to the changing nature of Internet links, the Rosen Publishing
Group, Inc., has developed an online list of Web sites related to the
subject of this book. This site is updated regularly. Please use this
link to access the list:

http://www.rosenlinks.com/lallp/uspa

FOR FURTHER READING

Egan, Tracie. *How a Bill Becomes a Law* (Primary Source Library of American Citizenship). New York, NY: Rosen Publishing Group, 2003.

Gilgannon, Denise, and Syl Sobel. *The U.S. Constitution and You.* Hauppauge, NY: Barron's Educational Series, 2001.

Innes, Brian. *International Terrorism* (Crime and Detection). Broomall, PA: Mason Crest Publishers, 2003.

Keeley, Jennifer. *Deterring and Investigating Attack*: The Role of the FBI and CIA (Library of Homeland Security). San Diego, CA: Lucent Books, 2003.

Margulies, Phillip. *Al-Qaeda: Osama bin Laden's Army of Terrorists* (Inside the World's Most Infamous Terrorist Organizations). New York, NY: Rosen Publishing Group, 2003.

Morris, Bruce, and Donna Wells. *Live Aware, Not in Fear: The 411 After 9-11, A Book for Teens.* Deerfield Beach, FL: HCI Teens, 2002.

National Commission on Terrorist Attacks. *The 9/11 Commission Report: Final Report of the National Commission on Terrorist Attacks upon the United States.* New York, NY: W. W. Norton & Company, 2004.

BIBLIOGRAPHY

American Civil Liberties Union. "Surveillance Under the USA
    Patriot Act." Retrieved July 2004 (http://www.aclu.org/
    SafeandFree/SafeandFree.cfm?ID=12263&c=206).

Barrett, Jennifer. "Promoting the Patriot Act." *Newsweek*, April 26,
    2004. Retrieved August 2004 (http://www.msnbc.msn.com/id/
    4839040/site/newsweek).

Bridis, Ted. "U.S. Court Approved 1,228 Special Terror Warrants Last
    Year." *San Francisco Chronicle*, May 1, 2003. Retrieved December
    22, 2004 (http://www.sfgate.com/cgi-bin/article.cgi?f=news/
    archive/2003/05/01/national1228EDT0624.DTL).

Clarke, Rachel. "Ashcroft Trumpets Anti-terror Laws." *BBC News
    Online*, August 20, 2003. Retrieved August 2004
    (http://news. bbc.co.uk/1/hi/world/americas/3164785.stm).

Eggen, Dan. "Key Part of Patriot Act Ruled Unconstitutional."
    Washington Post, September 30, 2004, p. A16.

Frieden, Terry. "Federal Judge Rules Part of Patriot Act
    Unconstitutional." CNN. January 24, 2004. Retrieved August
    2004 (http://www.cnn.com/2004/LAW/01/27/patriot.act).

McGee, Jim. "Bush Team Seeks Broader Surveillance Power."
    Washington Post, December 2, 2001, p. A 25.

Mitrano, Tracy. "Taking the Mystery out of the USA Patriot Act:
    Information, Process, and Protocol." Cornell University.
    October 14, 2003. Retrieved August 2004
    (http://www.cit.cornell.edu/oit/PatriotAct/article.html).

Mittelstadt, Michelle. "Patriot Act Available Against Many Types of
    Criminals." *Dallas Morning News*, September 7, 2003. Retrieved
    December 22, 2004 (http://www.centredaily.com/mld/
    centredaily/news/6716551.htm).

Murray, Frank J. "Patriot Act of 2001 Casts Wide Net." *Washington
    Times*, June 15, 2003. Retrieved December 22, 2004

(http://www.washingtontimes.com/functions/
print.php?StoryID=20030615-123422-5163r).

National Commission on Terrorist Attacks. *The 9/11 Commission
Report: Final Report of the National Commission on Terrorist
Attacks upon the United States.* New York, NY: W. W. Norton &
Company, 2004.

O'Harrow, Robert, Jr. "Six Weeks in Autumn." *Washington Post*,
October 27, 2002.

Schabner, Dean. "War on Terror Walkouts." ABC News. December
17, 2002. Retrieved August 2004 (http://abcnews.go.com/
sections/us/DailyNews/usapatriot_oakland021217.html).

U.S. Congress. House of Representatives. *Uniting and Strengthening
America by Providing Appropriate Tools Required to Intercept and
Obstruct Terrorism* (USA Patriot Act). H.R. 3162. 107th Cong., 1st
sess., October 24, 2001.

White House Transcript. "Address to a Joint Session of Congress and
the American People," September 20, 2001. Retrieved August
2004 (http://www.whitehouse.gov/news/releases/2001/09/
20010920-8.html).

White House Transcript. "President Calls for Renewing the USA
PATRIOT Act," April 19, 2004. Retrieved August 2004
(http://www.whitehouse.gov/news/releases/2004/04/
20040419-4.html).

Zetter, Kim. "The Patriot Act Is Your Friend." Wired News. February
24, 2004. Retrieved September 2004 (http://www.wired.com/
news/politics/0,1283,62388,00.html).

INDEX

About the Author

Bill Scheppler is an award-winning author who has researched and written extensively on the aftermath of the 9/11 tragedy, culminating in his books *Guantánamo Bay and Military Tribunals: Detention Center for Terrorists; Iraqi Insurgents: Iraqi Resistance to America After the Defeat of Saddam Hussein;* and his latest, *The USA Patriot Act: Antiterror Legislation in Response to 9/11.* Scheppler, who holds a BA degree in history, is currently researching his next project, a biography of celebrated medieval Muslim scholar and astronomer Abu Raihan al-Biruni. Scheppler resides in the San Francisco Bay Area with his wife, Emily.

Photo Credits

Cover, pp. 1, 3 © Royalty-Free/Corbis; p. 5 © Associated Press/ Department of Defense; pp. 7, 8, 12, 31 © Reuters/Corbis; pp. 10, 22, 24, 28, 36, 38 © Associated Press/Wide World Photos; p. 15 © Corbis Sygma; p. 17 © Joe Klein/Corbis; p. 18 © Tibor Bognar/Corbis; p. 19 © Ron Sachs/Corbis; p. 20 © Brooks Kraft/Corbis; p. 26 © AFP/ Getty Images, Inc.; p. 30 © Associated Press/Justice Department; p. 35 © Kevin Lamarque/Reuters/Corbis.

Designer: Thomas Forget; Editor: Kathy Kuhtz Campbell
Photo Researchers: Thomas Forget and Hillary Arnold